Clarinet Student

by
Fred Weber
in collaboration with
Robert Lowry

To The Student

Level II of the Belwin "Student Instrumental Course" is a continuation of Level I of this series or may be used to follow any other good elementary instruction book. It is designed to help you become an excellent player on your instrument in a most enjoyable manner. It will take a reasonable amount of work and CAREFUL practice on your part. If you do this, learning to play should be a valuable and pleasant experience.

Please see top of Page 3 for practice suggestions and other comments that should be very helpful.

To The Teacher

Level II of this series is a continuation of the Belwin "Student Instrumental Course", which is the first and only complete course for individual instruction of all band instruments. Like instruments may be taught in classes. Cornets, Trombones, Baritones and Basses may be taught together. The course is designed to give the student a sound musical background and, at the same time, provide for the highest degree of interest and motivation. The entire course is correlated to the band oriented sequence.

Each page of this book is planned as a complete lesson, however, because some students advance more rapidly than others, and because other lesson situations may vary, lesson assignments are left to the discretion of the teacher.

To make the course both authoritative and practical, most books are co-authored by a national authority of each instrument in collaboration with Fred Weber, perhaps the most widely-known and accepted authority at the student level.

The Belwin "Student Instrumental Course" has three levels: elementary, intermediate, and advanced intermediate. Each level consists of a method and three correlating supplementary books. In addition, a duet book is available for Flute, B♭ Clarinet, E♭ Alto Sax, B♭ Cornet and Trombone. The chart below shows the correlating books available with each part.

The Belwin "STUDENT INSTRUMENTAL COURSE" - A course for individual and class instruction of LIKE instruments, at three levels, for all band instruments.

EACH BOOK IS COMPLETE IN ITSELF BUT ALL BOOKS ARE CORRELATED WITH EACH OTHER

METHOD
"The B♭ Clarinet Student"
For individual or class instruction.

ALTHOUGH EACH BOOK CAN BE USED SEPARATELY, IDEALLY, ALL SUPPLEMENTARY BOOKS SHOULD BE USED AS COMPANION BOOKS WITH THE METHOD

STUDIES & MELODIOUS ETUDES	TUNES FOR TECHNIC	B♭ CLARINET SOLOS	DUETS FOR STUDENTS

Supplementary scales, warm-up and technical drills, musicianship studies and melody-like etudes, all carefully correlated with the method.	Technical type melodies, variations, and "famous passages" from musical literature for the development of — technical dexterity.	Four separate correlated Solos, with piano accompaniment, written or arranged by Robert Lowry:
		Cavelleria Rusticana...*Masagni*
		The Sioux Song and Dance..................... *Lowry*
		Valse and Volante...... *Lowry*
		Song and Prayer from "Hansel and Gretel".. *Humperdinck*
			A book of carefully correlated duet arrangements of interesting and familiar melodies without piano accompaniments.
			Available for: Flute
			                B♭ Clarinet
			                Alto Sax
			                B♭ Cornet
			                Trombone

CLARINET FINGERING CHART

How To Read The Chart

● - Indicates hole closed, or keys to be pressed.

○ - Indicates hole open.

When a number is given, refer to the picture of the Clarinet for additional key to be pressed.

When two notes are given together (F# and Gb), they are the same tone and, of course, played the same way.

When there are two or more fingerings given for a note, use the first one unless your teacher tells you otherwise.

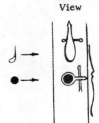

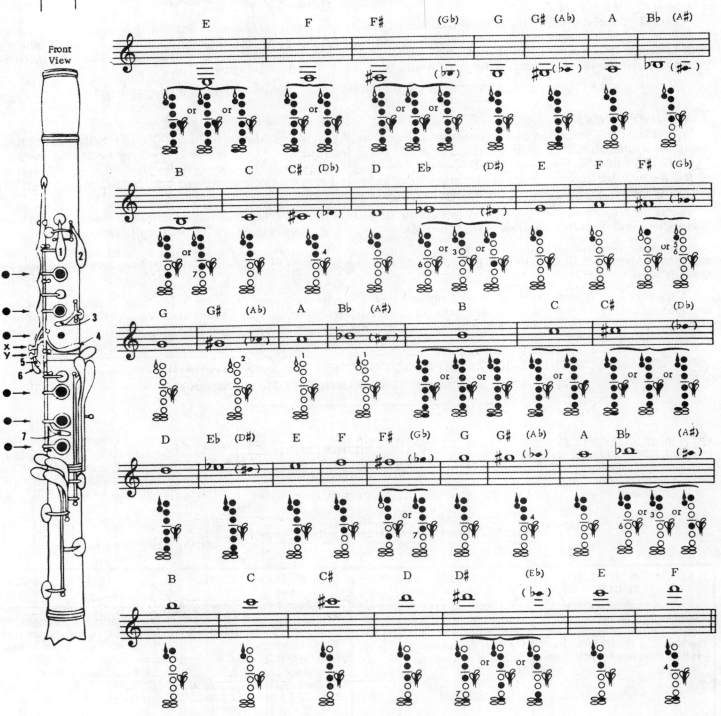

A Few Important Practice Suggestions

1. Set a regular practice time and make every effort to practice at this time.
2. ALWAYS practice carefully. Careless practice is a waste of time. Learn to play each line exactly as written. Later there may be times when certain freedoms may be taken.
3. ALWAYS use a *good* reed. When it is nicked or damaged in any way it should be discarded. The way to be economical with reeds is to take care of good reeds. Don't see how long you can still use them after they have been damaged.
4. The instrument must always be clean, in good playing condition, and all keys adjusted properly.
5. The development of careful and accurate playing habits is essential if you are to become a good player. Proper hand, finger, mouth or embouchure, and body position is absolutely necessary for best results. Always keep relaxed.
6. COUNT AT ALL TIMES.

Remember — Music should be fun but the better player you are the more
fun you have. It takes work to become a good player.

Daily Warm-Up Studies

The lines below are intended for use as daily warm-up drill, rhythm and dynamic studies, and for the development of technical proficiency. They should be used as an addition or supplement to the regular lesson assignment.

USE CERTAIN LINES as a daily routine with changes from time to time as suggested by your teacher.

Use the above tones in the following manner:

1. As long tones — Hold each note as long as comfortable. Listen carefully for your best tone and keep the tone steady.
2. Play each tone using various shadings as indicated in (a), (b), and (c) below. (number ②)
3. Use Pattern (d) (number ② below) on each scale tone — first staccato, then with accents.

Play slowly and listen carefully.

Key of C Major

Always try and play with your most pleasant sounding tone. Take lots of time while practicing Number 1 and listen carefully as you practice. Correct practicing of Number 1 should take much more time than any other study on the page.

Emperor Waltz

STRAUSS

If you have not already done so, please see the book "STUDIES AND MELODIOUS ETUDES FOR CLARINET" for more scale and technical studies that correlate with this Method Book.

Fingering Studies

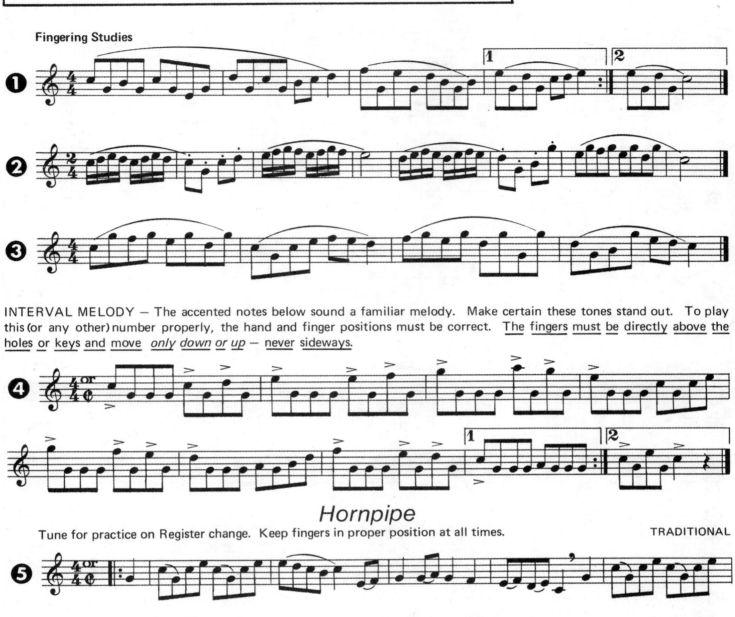

INTERVAL MELODY — The accented notes below sound a familiar melody. Make certain these tones stand out. To play this (or any other) number properly, the hand and finger positions must be correct. The fingers must be directly above the holes or keys and move *only down or up* — never sideways.

Hornpipe

Tune for practice on Register change. Keep fingers in proper position at all times.

TRADITIONAL

Nocturne

Play the regular notes the first time; then repeat an octave higher using cued notes.
Play as a song - with expression.

CHOPIN

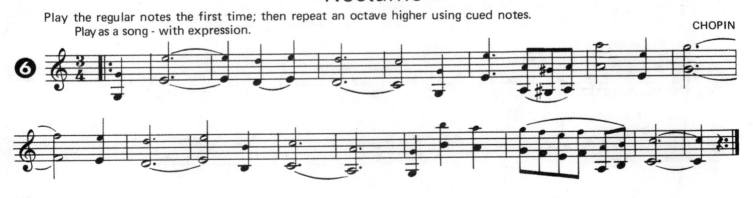

Please see the book "TUNES FOR CLARINET TECHNIC" for more melodies that provide further technical development.

Scale of F Major

Light and Separated

Scale and Articulation Study — Play all staccato notes lightly and separated.

simile

A *GRACE NOTE* is a very short note played lightly just before the main or accented note. In most grace note situations, the grace note is played just before the beat, with the main note coming on the beat. There is a variation of this but we aren't concerned with it at this time.

Grace Notes

Gavotte

Allegro moderato

GOSSEC

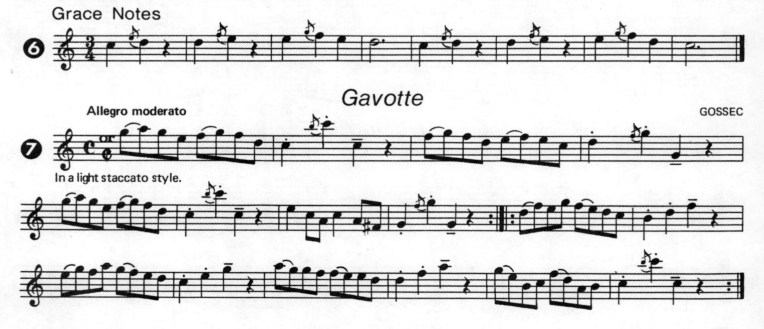

In a light staccato style.

1. *REMEMBER — Some notes on the clarinet can be fingered more than one way. These extra fingerings are usually called *alternate* fingerings. It is very important to know *how* and *when* to use these fingerings because they lead to faster and smoother playing as you progress. Their use is absolutely essential in more advanced clarinet playing.

2. This mark (∗) means use alternate fingering. When F♯ (or G♭) is played in a chromatic situation, approached by half steps, we use the alternate fingering for F♯. This is true of both octaves treated below. Another way to think of it is that when we go from F natural to F♯, or vice versa, we must use the alternate fingering for F♯.

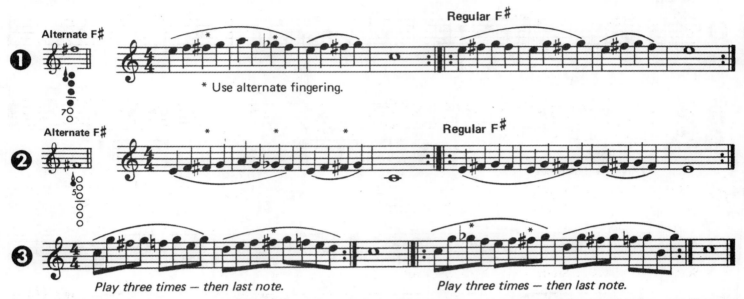

* Use alternate fingering.

Play three times — then last note.   *Play three times — then last note.*

3. When C♯ (third space) or (D♭) follows or precedes C natural, it is usually played with the <u>left</u> hand, little finger. Ask your teacher to show you the relationship between the keys played with the <u>little fingers</u> of <u>both hands</u> and how B, C, and C♯ can be played with either the right or left hand little fingers. The best general rule to remember, is that if one of these keys is used on one side, the next one must be on the other side. In other words, we alternate sides. You *never* slide across these little finger keys.

Practice both octaves.

* *See Page 40 for presentation of all common alternate fingerings.*

B.I.C.206

Review of Staccato

1. Staccato (dots) means to play notes <u>separated</u> or <u>spaced</u>. There must be a slight rest or silence between the notes. This is accomplished by a short stoppage of air between the notes. Accented notes are also separated. It helps in learning to play with separation to start playing notes slowly with a rest between each note, then speed up using the same style of playing. <u>Do</u> <u>not</u> <u>relax</u> <u>the</u> <u>embouchure</u> <u>position</u> <u>in</u> <u>any</u> <u>way</u>. Only the tongue moves.

2. We have what is called *syncopation* when the accented note comes between the main beats or counts of a measure. The longer note is usually stronger or accented.

Key of G

Review

1 D

G Scale

2

Thirds

simile

simile

Also use a continuous slur.

4

Scale and Counting Etude

5

Wedding Of The Winds

HALL

Waltz tempo

6

Review note on alternate fingerings, Page 7. When low B natural comes before or after B♭, it is played with the alternate fingering for B natural.

Alternate B♮

* Note alternate fingerings

①

Use regular E♮

Work out slowly, then speed up

②

③ Play 4 times.   Play 4 times.

④

Slow **6/8** (6 beats per measure) Practice both octaves.

⑤

Count 6 (♪ = 1 count)

Theme From Gypsy Baron

STRAUSS

Moderato

⑥

12

DUETS FOR STUDENTS is a book of carefully correlated duet arrangements of interesting and familiar melodies. Practicing these duets will improve your playing ability in a pleasant manner. It will also give you valuable experience in playing with others.

Fingering Drill

Write counting under notes, then play.

Etude

Barcarolle

OFFENBACH

6 counts per measure.(♪ = 1 count)

To next strain

Fine ending

Fine

D.C. al Fine

Work out slowly, then try for speed.

Also slur every two notes

On Wings Of Song

MENDELSSOHN

14

Arpeggio Etude — Work out slowly, then speed up.

❶

Fine

D. C. al Fine

Etude

❷

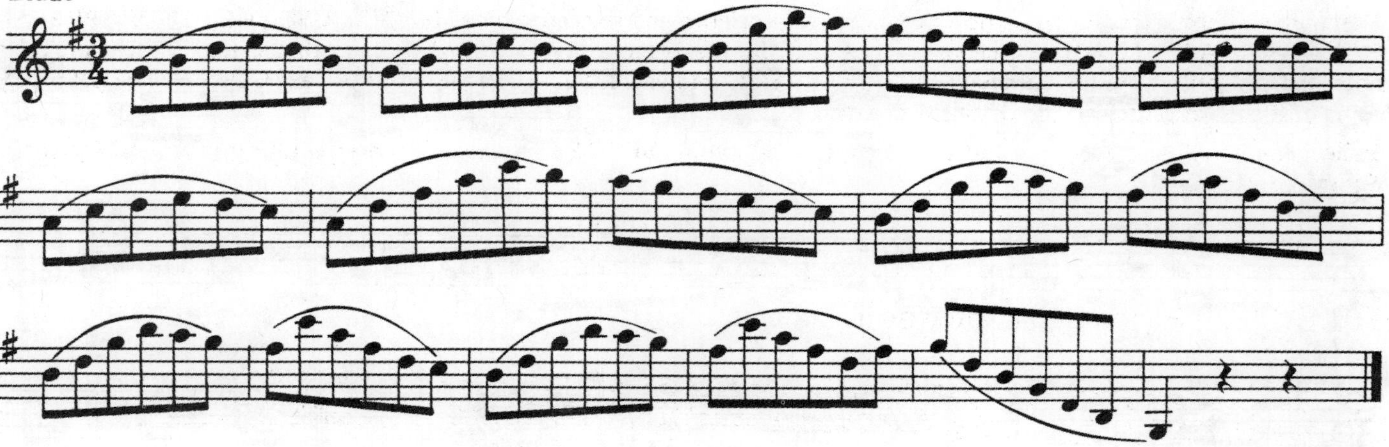

Sonatina

BEETHOVEN

Moderato

❸ *mp*

Fine

f

rit.
D. C. al Fine

B.I.C.206

Etude

A Counting Tune

Red River Valley

There are numerous ways to learn how to count dotted eighth and sixteenth notes (♪. ♫). USE THE SYSTEM PREFERRED BY YOUR TEACHER. This procedure is suggested by the author: Think DOWN - UP with the foot on the dotted eighth note, the sixteenth note being played after the UP beat, midway between the UP and the next DOWN. The UP beat MUST come in the exact center or middle of the count.

Sometimes it helps to think of the sixteenth note as coming BEFORE the note it precedes rather than AFTER the dotted eighth it follows.

Dotted Eighth and Sixteeth Notes

Count: 1   2   3

Country Gardens

P. GRAINGER

Play the above pattern on all tones of the C and G Scales (from memory).

Light and separated

Sometimes abbreviations are used in writing music. In the line below a BAR across the stem means to divide the note into eighth notes.(two BARS would mean Sixteenth notes). Frequently, but not always, dots are used to indicate how many tones the note is divided into.

Cielito Linda

A Tonguing Tune — fast

Dance From The Nutcracker Suite

Light Staccato Style — Count carefully.

TSCHAIKOWSKY

rit.

Prelude

Andante

CHOPIN

Play each 3 times, then last note.

Play 4 times.

Work out slowly, then increase speed.

Andante Cantabile

MENDELSSOHN

Slow 6/8 — (count 6)

Stars And Stripes Forever

SOUSA

Briskly

Trio

If counting gives trouble, work out first in 4/4 time.

* Alt. Fing.

Chromatic Etude

Counting Rests

When a piece in 6/8 time goes quite fast, it is difficult to count out all 6 beats. We simplify this on 6/8 tunes that are played fast by counting only 2 counts per measure. In this book, pieces in which we count out all 6 beats will be referred to as SLOW 6/8, and those we count in 2 beats per measure will be FAST 6/8. The counting written under the notes in the line below shows you the comparison between counting slow and fast 6/8 time. You will note that in FAST 6/8 time there are 3 eighth notes (♪♪♪) to a beat and a ♩. receives one beat.

Practice in both slow and fast 6/8

Sailing Sailing

Fast 6/8 — 2 beats per measure

Low Notes

Practice both fingerings

2 beats per measure — practice slowly, then increase speed.

Fine

D. C. al Fine

Sailor's Hornpipe

Practice slowly, then increase speed

TRADITIONAL

Keep fingers in proper positions at all times.

Arpeggio Waltz

Minuet

J. S. BACH

Irish Washerwoman

JIG

Minor Scales

There is a minor scale corresponding with every major scale and having the same key signature. By starting on the 6th tone of a major scale, using the same key signature and playing an octave, we have a minor scale. Although there are three forms of the minor scale, only two forms, harmonic and melodic are frequently used. The *harmonic* form follows the key signature except the 7th tone is raised one-half step both going up and coming down. In the melodic minor scale, the 6th and 7th scale tones are raised one-half step from what is indicated in the key signature when going up. Coming down it follows the key signature.

Both the harmonic and melodic forms of minor are used below in the three most common minor keys. Practice and study them carefully so you understand how they are formed. Try to become familiar with their sound.

See chart Page 2 for fingering

Minor Etudes

a minor

Russian Sailor Dance

Key of B♭

B♭ Scale

❶

Practice both octaves *See note at bottom of next page.*

❷

Play bottom octave first time — top octave on repeat.   *Play top octave first time — and bottom octave on repeat.*
Use various articulations as suggested in the first measure.

simile

❸

simile

❹

Vilia Song

Many clarinet players can play a lot of notes rapidly. However, the true test of a good player is whether or not he can play a song-like melody with beauty, style, proper expression and phrasing. On all song-like melodies work primarily to achieve beauty, expression, and a singing quality. Don't just play notes.

LEHAR

Gracefully   **Phrasing Line**

❺

Use soft tongue stroke

Eb

On repeat — play all high E's — Eb

Triplets

March From The Nutcracker Suite

TSCHAIKOWSKY

Key of D

27

Work out slowly, then speed up.

Soldier's Joy

TRADITIONAL

① *Play three times, then last note.*   *Repeat 3 times*   *Repeat 3 times*

Chromatic
②

③

Etude in g minor
④

Trio

National Emblem March

BAGLEY

⑤

1

2

Practice fingering B — C in two ways.

Emphasize accented notes

Counting Etude
Majestically

4

Garry Owen

Work out slowly, then speed up.

JIG

5

Etude

Etude

Gopak

Lively

RUSSIAN FOLK DANCE

Fine

D. C. al Fine

B.I.C.206

Octaves
Very slow — **legato.** Listen carefully

Melody Etude — Work out slowly, then speed up.

This arpeggio Etude is based on the melody of *"Brahms Lullaby".* Work it out carefully and then speed up. Emphasize the accented notes.

Arpeggios On Brahms' Lullaby

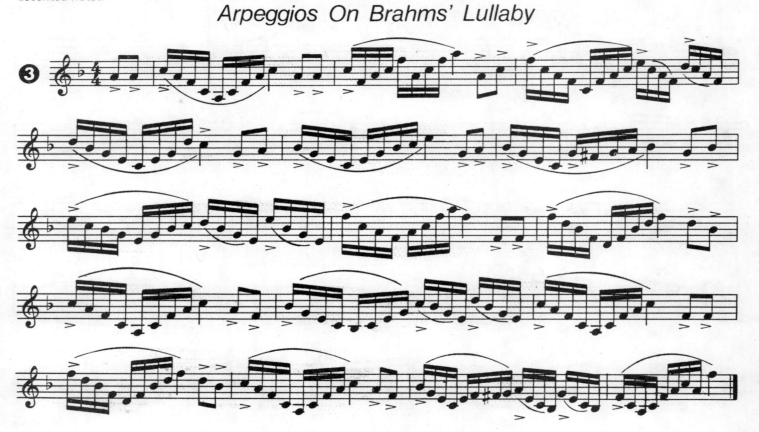

Minor Scales
Review note on Page 22.

Relative Minor to B♭ Major
g minor *(Harmonic Form)*

❶

g minor *(Melodic Form)*

❷

❸

Relative Minor to D Major
b minor *(Harmonic Form)*

❹ Like B♭

b minor *(Melodic Form)*

❺

❻

Minor Etude

❼ *p*

Fine p

mp   *f*   *D.S. al Fine*

Note Speller   1. Name Note.   2. Mark Fingering.

34

Tonguing Etude

b minor Counting Etude

Hungarian Dance No. 4

In g minor
With expression

BRAHMS

Count: +   2   +   1

Lively, with spirit

Like Bb

B.I.C.206

Key of Eb
Eb Scale

Poem

FIBICH

6 beats per measure
Slowly

Counting Tune — Work out counting carefully, then play at a moderate tempo.

Fine

D. S. al Fine.

The Jolly Swiss Boy

Fine

D. C. al Fine

1 *Play three times, then last note.*   *Play three times, then last note.*   *Play three times, then last note.*

Chromatic

2

3

Slowly

4

Hungarian Dance No. 6

BRAHMS

With vigor

5

Etude

Oh Susanna

A Tonguing and Counting Tune

FOSTER

Swan Lake

Moderato with expression

TSCHAIKOWSKY

Key Of A

A Scale Fill in — The sharped notes are , , and .

Play bottom octave first time — top octave on repeat.

Play top octave first time — bottom octave on repeat.

R L R
L R L

Spanish Dance

MOSZKOWSKI

Practice first without grace notes..

Fine

D. C. al Fine

Play three times, then last note.　Play three times, then last note.　Play three times, then last note.

Tonguing Low Notes

Etude

Fine　D. C.

Waltz From Coppelia

DELIBES

Variation On An Old Theme

Work out slowly, then speed up.

Minuet

BOCCHERINI

Not too fast

Count: 3   1 + 2 + 3 +   1 etc.

rit.   a tempo

c minor *(Melodic Form)* — Relative to E♭ Major

Hurricane

Very fast — in strict tempo

Fine

D. C. al Fine

f♯ minor *(Melodic Form)* — Relative to A Major

Melodies From Hungarian Rhapsody No. 2

Work out carefully, then play in a vigorous manner.

LISZT

Repeat must be played.

simile

Fast Tonguing Etude

❶

p

Etude

❷

Fine

D. C. al Fine

Won't You Come Home Bill Bailey?
Arranged

Technic (a-la-Dixieland)

❸ Ⓐ

f

Ⓑ

Key of A♭

A♭ Scale

Play bottom octave first time — top octave on repeat   *Play top octave first time — bottom octave on repeat*

Caprice

Valse

Slow waltz tempo

CHOPIN

Count: 3 1 2 3

Chromatic

①

Etude in f minor

②

Etude — Work out slowly

③

Pizzicato Polka

DELIBES

Play in light, staccato manner.

④

mf

Fine

D. S. al Fine

This page is intended to give the student an introductory knowledge and understanding of scales, scale structure and keys. The teacher is encouraged to expand on these ideas as he sees fit.

Scales and Keys

We are frequently told to practice scales because it will make us better players. Practicing scales improves our finger dexterity; But there is another and probably more important reason.

A piece of music in a certain key is usually based on the scale containing the same sharps or flats. For instance, a tune in the key of F (1 flat in the key signature) is usually based on the scale of F which contains one flat. This relationship with the scale is the same for ALL keys. As we learn to play each scale, a certain fingering pattern is developed which greatly increases our ability to play in the key based on that scale. Our fingers grow accustomed to the fingering pattern of the key.

Since on a wind instrument there is no way of showing a complete picture of all the notes and their relationship to each other, the drawing of a piano or organ key board showing all the notes is printed below.

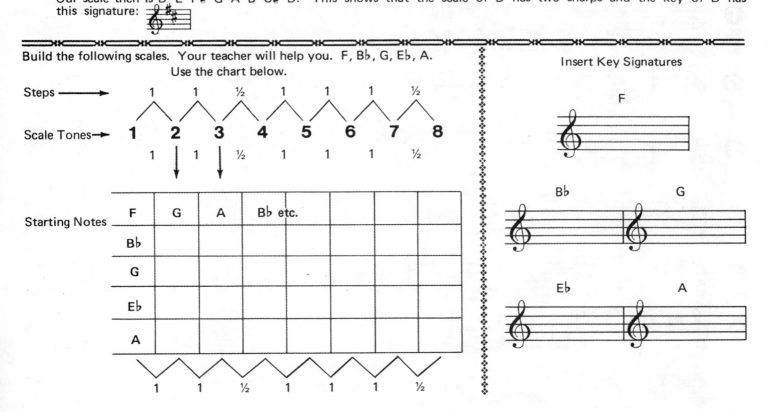

Memorize

1. A half-step is the distance from any note to the closest note above or below, regardless of whether it is a black key or white key.
2. A whole-step is two half-steps.
3. ALL scales follow a definite pattern of half-steps and whole-steps.

The MAJOR scale is the most common scale and the only one we can be concerned with on this page. The major scale always follows this pattern of half-steps and whole-steps. *(notes of the scale)* 1 2 3 4 5 6 7 8

Steps between — — 1 1 ½ 1 1 1 ½

From this, you can see the half and whole-step pattern. 1 1 ½ 1 1 1 ½ (2 whole steps and a half-step followed by 3 whole-steps and a half-step).

Each major scale has 8 tones and is one octave. It can be repeated over several octaves either down or up. From the keyboard diagram you can see that the scale starting on "C" follows this pattern without using any sharps or flats. This is why the scale of C and the key of C has no sharps or flats.

Scales can be started on any tone of the keyboard. By building <u>alphabetically</u> according to the major scale pattern of half and whole-steps (1 1 ½ 1 1 1 ½), a major scale is formed.

EXAMPLE: Start on D–a whole-step above D is E — another whole-step is F♯ — a half-step up is G. A whole-step up is A— another whole-step is B and the next whole-step is C♯. We complete the scale with a half-step to D.

Our scale then is D E F♯ G A B C♯ D. This shows that the scale of D has two sharps and the key of D has this signature:

Build the following scales. Your teacher will help you. F, B♭, G, E♭, A. Use the chart below.

Insert Key Signatures

Scales

The Scale patterns below provide unlimited scale and articulation practice in the seven most common band keys. Start with ANY number and play through the entire pattern, returning to the starting line and playing to where END is marked. End by holding the last note. KEEP THE STARTING KEY THROUGHOUT THE ENTIRE PATTERN. Use various articulations.

Chromatics

Flight Of The Bumble Bee
A Chromatic Piece

This number is presented as a challenge for chromatic development.   Work out carefully then try for speed with accuracy.

RIMSKY · KORSAKOV

Alternate Fingerings

The most common alternate fingerings are shown below, together with examples of when they are to be used. Even though it may take some effort to learn how and when to use them, their use will greatly increase your ability to play rapidly and smoothly when you play faster and more difficult music. Master their use — it will pay big dividends later.

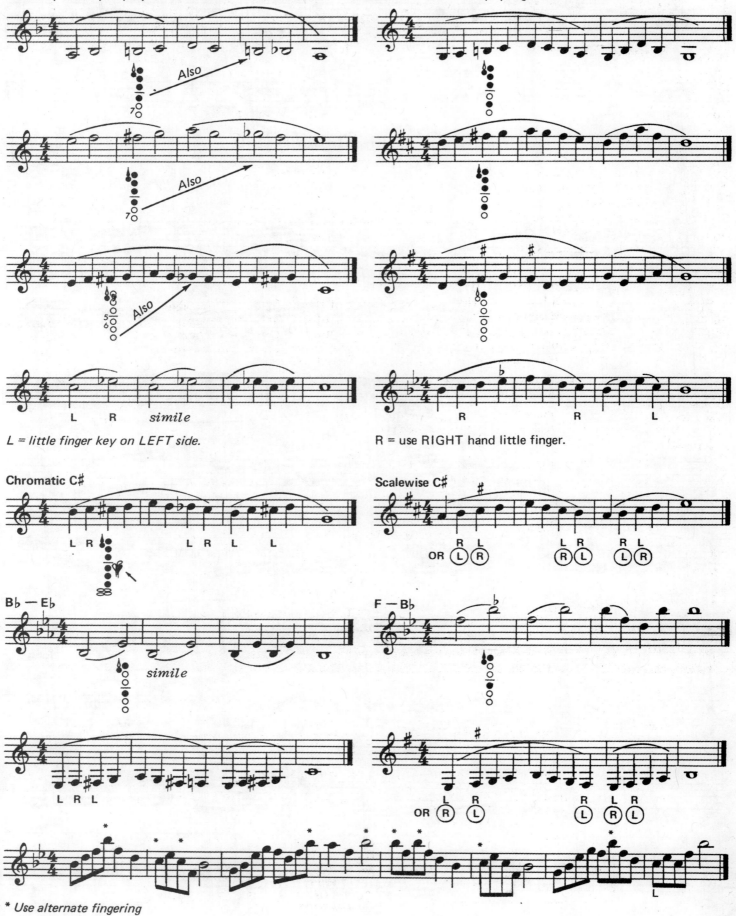

L = little finger key on LEFT side.

R = use RIGHT hand little finger.

Chromatic C#

Scalewise C#

Bb — Eb

F — Bb

* Use alternate fingering